Young at Heart

The Step-By-Step Way of Writing Children's Stories

Violet Ramos

D1366839

VR Publications
Scottsdale, Arizona

Young at Heart
The Step-By-Step Way of Writing Children's Stories
By Violet Ramos

Published by: VR Publications
                 P.O. Box 4643
                 Scottsdale, Arizona 85261
                 E-Mail: vrpubs@uswest.net

10 9 8 7 6 5 4 3 2

Library of Congress Cataloging in Publication Data:

YOUNG AT HEART: The Step-By-Step Way of Writing Children's Stories / by Violet Ramos.

Library of Congress Card Number 98-91058
ISBN 0-9658334-1-0 (pbk)

Second Edition.
Printed in the U.S.A.

This book is designed to provide helpful information on how to write children's stories. It is based on the views and opinions of the author.

It is written in a simple way that motivates creativity. It encourages writers to use their unique style of writing to develop a story for children. It does not in any way guarantee a publishing house will buy a story.

You are urged to read all of the material, learn as much as possible, and apply each step to your own writing. Each step is a building block to writing a children's story.

Every effort has been made to make this manual as complete and accurate as possible for the writer who wants to achieve greater creative freedom.

Contents

Acknowledgments

I would like to thank all of my students, throughout the years, for their encouragement and feedback in my teaching methods. It is through their suggestions that this book was created.

Thanks also to Ray for his valued suggestions and, of course, my daughter Catherine, who spends endless hours reading every manuscript I write, from its creation until the finished product is put to print.

Preface

Creating a story is a freedom of words. Through your thoughts you form words that project your feelings to the readers of your book. It is fun and it is stimulating, but most important, it is unique because it comes from you.

This book is written in a very simple format. It is structured to let your creativity flow. It will alleviate much of the intimidation that most people feel about being creative. If you follow step by step, you will develop your own style of putting a story together. It is that simple. You will have a great time letting the child within you talk for you.

Each step provides you with an example, exercise, and a worksheet for your convenience. It is important you study each example then complete each exercise before you go on to the next step.

The "Notes from the Author" section preceding each step relates how the author's experiences and opinions influence the development of a story. Each was written to encourage all writers to reach down deep and write with no inhibitions.

Try to forget, for a few moments, spelling, punctuation, and sentence structure; just let your ideas flow onto paper. Let your creativity take you into a wonderful world of make-believe. Go back to your childhood and think as a child. Put your thoughts down on paper with no hesitation. Think of your story as a few moments of reading or learning pleasure for young children.

Overall, this book provides a valuable and exciting process for writing.

About the Author

In over 12 years, Violet Ramos has taught hundreds of students how to release their creativity into children's stories. She feels there is a child in everyone who wants to speak out and reach other children.

Ramos believes that simplicity is the key that opens the door to creativity. This book is written in a very simple format so that it takes the reader very little effort to write a story for children of all ages. Ramos' theory relies on her experience that the story begins when the words start to flow on paper. The plot or events that keep the reader's attention are the writer's own accumulation of experiences.

Although Ramos has taught in four states—Texas, Virginia, Maryland, and now Arizona she hopes to reach more writers by publishing *Young at Heart: The Step-By-Step Way of Writing Children's Stories.*

She believes that everyone has a story to tell and they should write it in their own unique style.

Cover and Interior design by Lisa Liddy, The Printed Page, Phoenix Arizona.

✒ Notes from the Author

As a young child, I always recognized the importance of school. I learned the rules of grammar that had been established years before, but I must admit I didn't accept them willingly. When I am releasing creativity, I find proper sentence structure, punctuation, and spelling are too restrictive to my flow of thoughts.

As a free thinker, even at a very young age, I could not understand why you couldn't step out of bounds and let your thoughts create. What difference did it make, as long as you created something useful and beautiful for others to enjoy. I still feel that way, perhaps even more strongly because I am no longer a child. Yet I am very proud to say I still have a child within me. It is this child that helps me write children's stories freely and in my own style.

You may choose to write about events of today or those of yesterday. You may even want to write about events that took place in your own childhood or you may write about something you heard from a friend or person in passing. It really doesn't matter because your imagination will take control of the words when you start your exercises. ⚜

Step One: Main Character

The main character is very important. It is the predominant character in a story. Your main character can be anything; a cloud, a raindrop, early morning dew on a rose petal, a roaring lion, a tweeting bird, a mooing cow, or a sassy little boy or girl. Let your imagination decide for you. What a great opportunity to release your imagination and let it be totally free.

Example

Sara was a happy little girl until she lost Spark. Spark was her little dog. Spark kept her warm at night. Every day, Spark sat at Sara's feet while she ate her meals. Sara loved Spark very much! Now Sara was alone.

Exercise

Write a brief paragraph with a main character. I will make it easy for you this time. I will give you two main characters to choose from, either a tired old car plugging along down a winding dirt road or a wilting rose in need of water.

Let your imagination develop your main character into someone special with a unique personality. Let your feelings and emotions pour into your main character.

Here is the perfect time to challenge and expand your creativity. It may cause a little anxiety, just at first, but step out of the bounds and release your imagination into the wonderful world of make believe.

To help with your flow of creativity, close your eyes for a few minutes, totally relax, and, if possible, don't think. After a brief period visualize your story before putting the words on paper.

Then let the words flow. They may not make sense at first but there will be a story within the words before you finish. Often you will find a combination of words that will start another creative story.

Write a paragraph using one main character, then stop and read your words. What an interesting main character a car or a wilting rose will make!

Worksheet

_____

_____

_____

_____

_____

_____

_____

_____

_____

_____

_____

_____

_____

_____

_____

_____

_____

_____

_____

Worksheet

_____

_____

_____

_____

_____

_____

_____

_____

_____

_____

_____

_____

_____

Very good, you have just developed a **Main Character.** Through your creativity you gave a car or a rose feelings and a personality. **Do not** change the personality you developed; it was developed totally free of any restrictions.

Notes from the Author

I have always sought to find meaning in everything. Every story I write has a message. Many times I write with no message in mind but before I finish there is a message. And then there are times when I start a story with a particular message and a different message will surface. I could blame my creativity or imagination, but I like to think it is the child within me having its own way.

As you write for children always remember there is a child who can either learn from your message or relate to the experiences you are describing in your story. Even if you write educational stories you will still have a message for your reader.

The difficulty in writing children's stories is that your message is coming from a "grownup" and you have to write a big message for little children. If you are writing for very young children, you will need to use only one or two very simple words to express a very important message. Though it may look easy, it is not. Try to think and feel as a child and surrender to your creativity. Let yourself feel the freedom, as a mature adult, in a make-believe world and have fun while you create a story with a message. 🌸

Step Two: Message

Messages come in surprise packages and you never know when they are going to emerge. When I was a child, the most important part of the story was the message. Once the message was obvious my reaction would always be, "Oh, I like that!"

Regardless of what you are writing, there will always be a message. The message is the purpose of your story. You want to share with the reader something special that only you can relay in your own style.

Your message can be anything, it can even be happy or sad. It is a learning lesson for children. A message must be totally honest from the writer's point of view, even if it is told in a wonderland script.

Your main character carries the message throughout your story. If you find that you have more than one message in your story decide on only one. It is too confusing for young children to have more than one message in a story.

You will never run out of ideas for messages. There are too many events happening everyday. Even a quiet, lonely day could be used to show children how to appreciate the little things around them. It is always helpful to keep a list of anything that you find interesting or important enough to write about in your stories. Once you write an idea down on paper, you can release it but you haven't lost it. You leave room in your thoughts for new ideas to develop.

Message List

_____   _____

_____   _____

_____   _____

_____   _____

_____   _____

_____   _____

_____   _____

_____   _____

_____   _____

_____   _____

_____   _____

_____   _____

_____   _____

_____   _____

_____   _____

_____   _____

Example

> *Sara was a happy little girl until she **lost Spark.*** *Spark was her little dog. **Spark was Sara's special friend.** Spark kept Sara warm at night. Every day, Spark sat at Sara's feet while she ate her meals. Sara loved Spark very much! **Now Sara was sad and alone.***

The message in my example is **friends bring happiness.**

Exercise

The focus in this exercise is the message. Start writing with a message in mind; use any thought you desire. Release your creativity and let it form words on paper. The first word is the most difficult because you are not in control! Your imagination is in control of you.

You will have the beginning of a totally creative story with a main character and a message. It will be brief but you can build on it. Sometimes it helps to have a smile on your face. However, if that isn't natural, go ahead and frown.

You are starting with a specific message, but the message may change before you finish writing the paragraph. It will be interesting to see if you have the same message when you complete the story.

Worksheet

_____

_____

_____

_____

_____

_____

_____

_____

_____

_____

_____

_____

_____

_____

_____

_____

_____

_____

_____

Worksheet

_____

_____

_____

_____

_____

_____

_____

_____

_____

_____

_____

_____

_____

_____

_____

_____

_____

_____

_____

_____

_____

Notes from the Author

I find that as a writer I spend many hours alone. I need the time to organize my thoughts and words. It may seem like I am a loner, but I am not because I thoroughly enjoy the company of other people. I once lived by myself, way out in the country high on a hill. It was beautiful and inspiring and lonely; I need people to keep every day interesting.

My love for people stems from my curiosity of personalities. Individuals are so very interesting. They have their own opinions and character traits making an interesting blend of personalities when grouped together.

I learned that in my writing it works the same way. The more characters I have in a story, the more interesting it becomes. A main character is needed in a story, but the main character needs supporting characters to help enforce the message and also to make the main character's personality predominant.

The fun part of developing supporting characters is that you can draw from the many people you have encountered in your life. Although each supporting character's role is different, they are essential in making the story complete.

Step Three: Supporting Characters

You will have supporting characters in your story, too. How many will depend on you, as the creator. The supporting characters will help make your main character more predominant, and they will also help to enforce your message.

Example:

*Sara was a happy little girl until she lost **Spark**. **Spark** was her little dog. **Spark** was Sara's special friend. **Spark** kept Sara warm at night. Every day, **Spark** sat at Sara's feet while she ate her meals. Sara loved **Spark** very much! Now Sara was sad and alone. One day Sara thought she saw **Spark** sitting in her special chair in the living room. It made Sara smile.*

Example: Car

*The tired old car plugged along down the winding dirt road. Not looking where it was going it drove over a sharp rock. The car started going bumpity-bump, swerving all over the road. The car started to slow down knowing the rear **tire** was going flat.*

*The **tire** looked up at the big frame over its head and said, "I am hurt, why don't you stop?"*

Or

Example: Rose

*The old flower bent over limp in the hot sun. "A sprinkle of water would help my thirst," she said weakly. "I want to stay strong for one more birthday party but I don't think I will make it." As the flower closed its petals to rest, a **cloud** blew over its head.*

*"Well, I can see I have my work cut out for me today. Every place I look it is dry, dry, dry. Wow, that old flower down there really needs my attention." Shaking and rumbling, the gray **cloud** sprinkled water on the petals of the old flower.*

Exercise

It is now time for you to write a new story with a main character, a message, and a supporting character. Use only one supporting character and only animals in this exercise. In one of my examples, I used a little girl and a dog. That is very simple. But if I used a pig for a main character and a mouse for a supporting character, wouldn't that story be interesting? Think of all the possibilities I would have to motivate the reader's imagination. There could be surprises and suspense.

Worksheet

Worksheet

_____

_____

_____

_____

_____

_____

_____

_____

_____

_____

_____

_____

_____

_____

_____

_____

_____

_____

_____

_____

_____

_____

_____

🖋 Notes from the Author

A writer's world is based on words. You have only the written word to communicate your story to the reader. You relate feelings and actions through words, just like you do when you speak. Every time you talk your personality is projected to your listener. The words you use and the way you use them tell the listener what type of personality you have. If my eyes are closed and you talk to me, I will form a mental picture of you from your words.

In writing a story the vocabulary you give your characters to communicate with one another is called dialogue. One of the most important uses of dialogue is the development and projection of a personality. You can actually turn a bird into a cowboy or a falling leaf into a Southern belle. You can have a wonderful time with dialogue making a story funny, sad, scary, and even gentle for the reader. And it takes so few words.

For instance, if I were to use the word "yeah," over and over again in a conversation with you, a mental picture of my personality would form quickly, and yet, it is just one word. Just think what you can do with an entire story by skillfully and selectively using dialogue. 🌿

Step Four: Dialogue

Writing dialogue is an opportunity to become an actor. Have fun with it. Develop different personalities with it. Act out the parts of your characters by talking on paper.

Here are a few descriptive combinations. Opposite the words listed below write a brief description of the character using the dialogue. Develop different personalities with it.

"You all."

"Oh, dear."

"You there."

"Hi doc."

"I'm strong."

Use dialogue when you want a personality to contribute to action and interest in the story. Remember, though, that it is a forceful tool in writing; use it directly and with caution. Too much dialogue can be boring for the reader.

Example

Sara was a happy little girl until she lost Spark. Spark was her little dog. Spark was Sara's special friend. Spark kept Sara warm at night. Every day, Spark sat at Sara's feet while she ate her meals. Sara loved Spark very much! Now Sara was sad and alone. Sara cried, "Oh Spark, where have you gone?"

One day Sara thought she saw Spark sitting in her special chair in the living room. It made Sara smile. The next day when Sara was eating lunch on the porch, she pretended to talk to Spark. All of a sudden she stopped and listened. Sara could hear Spark barking. She called, "Here Spark! Here Spark! Where are you?" Spark barked, "Woof, Woof."

Exercise

Visualize **a moon** for your main character and **a star** for your supporting character. After you have mentally formed your characters, start writing. Use creative dialogue to give each character a distinct personality. You can project whether your character lives on a farm or in the city, their education level, nationality and even age. In libraries you can find books on languages for different cultures. Keep your own list of accents and expressions as you talk to different people.

Accents and Expressions List

_____	_____
_____	_____
_____	_____
_____	_____
_____	_____
_____	_____
_____	_____
_____	_____
_____	_____
_____	_____
_____	_____
_____	_____
_____	_____
_____	_____
_____	_____
_____	_____

Worksheet

_____

_____

_____

_____

_____

_____

_____

_____

_____

_____

_____

_____

_____

_____

_____

_____

_____

_____

_____

_____

_____

Worksheet

_____

_____

_____

_____

_____

_____

_____

_____

_____

_____

_____

_____

_____

_____

_____

_____

_____

_____

_____

_____

_____

Notes from the Author

I have always tried to find something new and interesting to do; it is my way of staying away from routine. I consider routine, in any form, a dungeon of boredom. Even when reading a book, if the first chapter doesn't have an underlying sense of intrigue, I will put the book down.

You should want your book to be totally interesting and not easily put aside for another day. Most of the best-selling books grab the reader in the first few pages and do not let go until the book is finished. It isn't by accident that the story holds the interest of the reader; it is due to the skill of the author. An outstanding author knows how to use every tool of writing, especially those that are not obvious to the reader.

Contrast is one of those tools. Contrast is used throughout every story. It is used in characters, dialogue, and movement. It can be subtle or it can be extreme. It is not always obvious to the eye that contrast exists, but there is something that causes interest in the story. It is so important to a story that without it a story would just be a run of words.

I have always had a contrasting life full of activities. That is what you want to do with your story. It should be almost like a roller coaster, up and down and around, and at the end there is a smile on the reader's face. ❧

Step Five: Contrast

Contrast shows a difference in the events, actions, and emotions in a story. Your main character can be happy walking down a hall, when suddenly she feels a gust of cold air against her skin. The contrast of happy and cold alerts the reader that something is going to happen. Music achieves the same feeling in a movie. Keep contrast flowing throughout your story, especially with your dialogue.

When writing for very young children, remember that a child's attention span is very short and you must keep their interest until the end of the story. It takes skill in selecting words that develop contrast in a simple way. With practice your skill will improve. Contrast of words and situations helps to make a story exciting.

Example

*Sara was a **happy** little girl until she **lost** Spark. Spark was her little dog. Spark was Sara's special friend. Spark kept Sara **warm** when the **cold** wind blew at night. Every day, Spark sat at Sara's feet while she ate her meals in the big **drafty** kitchen. Sara loved Spark very much! Sara wasn't **happy** any more. Now*

*Sara was **sad** and **alone**. Sara cried, "Oh Spark, where have you gone?"*

*One day Sara thought she saw Spark sitting in her special chair in the living room. It made Sara **smile** instead of **cry**. The next day when Sara was eating lunch on the porch, she pretended to **talk** to Spark, so she wouldn't feel lonely. All of a sudden she stopped and **listened**. Sara could hear Spark barking. She called, "Here Spark! Here Spark! Where are you?" Spark barked, "Woof, Woof."*

The more you write, the more you will study the words when you read, and it will be obvious where the author used contrast. You will never again just read a story, you will observe as you read, unless you make an effort to turn off your writer's eye.

Before you go on to the next exercise, look at the following paragraph. Can you pick out the contrasts?

"They walked in scary alleys with shadows of gloom, where black cats hissed and leaped, running behind barrels of trash. By the shining light from far above, Sara and her Grandmother searched for anything they could use. When they were through, Sara and her Grandmother Rose carried their sacks all alone."

If you picked out the following words you were right.

gloom	**walk**	**scary**	**hissed**
light	**shadows**	**trash**	**leaped**

Exercise

Start a new story. Turn a happy afternoon into a cold, windy night. Make sure you include the following elements in your story:

🐦 A main character

🐦 A message

🐦 A supporting character

🐦 Dialogue

🐦 Contrast

Let the words flow freely for a time. Then go back and insert contrast.

You're still working with your total creativity. Do not worry about spelling, punctuation, sentence structure, or even story line; just let the words flow. Enjoy the total freedom of your imagination.

Worksheet

_____

_____

_____

_____

_____

_____

_____

_____

_____

_____

_____

_____

_____

_____

_____

_____

_____

_____

_____

_____

_____

Worksheet

_____

_____

_____

_____

_____

_____

_____

_____

_____

_____

_____

_____

_____

_____

_____

_____

_____

_____

_____

Notes from the Author

When I was growing up we moved often. Even after I was married we moved from air base to air base. I found a certain adventure in waking up in a strange room, using a new kitchen, and making new friends. Only nature seemed to stay the same. The sun, moon, even the birds sounded the same but the surroundings and neighborhoods were very different.

Moving is more than just plopping down in a new place. It is a constant growth of events. Because of my childhood, I grew to expect movement in my life. If time doesn't march on I feel like my surroundings become stagnant.

When writing a story it is also important to move your readers along into different segments of the story. It will motivate the reader's interest and imagination. Movement is a vehicle that will help you keep your reader's total attention.

You will have fun with movement because it will push you along, too. Once your creativity starts to roll out on paper, you want to let it continue to move. The more it moves, the more room you will have for new ideas. Your story will move along quickly and it will stay original in its ideas. ❧

Step Six: Movement

Like most things in life creativity does not stand still. Yours has moved right along. Your story should not stand still either. If your story does not have movement, what will prompt your reader to turn the page? It is up to you, as the writer, to keep the events in your story moving. Movement will keep the interest of your reader. Your writing skill will help the reader to move along with you. In using movement you can cover the age of your character by using events in your character's life such as attending different levels of school. You can show movement by using the different seasons of the year. You can also show movement by aging the dialogue of a specific character. If your characters are moving along in a car, use the stationary landmarks such as mountains or buildings. You can even show movement by using day and night.

It is easier to use movement with illustrations. Your illustrations can do the moving for you. Illustrations do not eliminate the need for words; they make movement easier to see.

When they were through, Sara and her Grandmother Rose carried their sacks all alone.

Example

*Sara was a happy little girl until she lost Spark one **day** when she was out **walking**. Spark was her little dog. Spark was Sara's special friend. Spark kept Sara warm and cozy when the cold wind **blew** at **night**. Every day, Spark sat at Sara's feet while she ate her meals in the big drafty kitchen and sometimes in the big formal dining room. Sara loved Spark very much! Sara wasn't happy any more. Now Sara was sad and alone as she **walked from room to room**. Sara cried, "Oh Spark, where have you gone?"*

*One day Sara thought she saw Spark sitting in her special chair in the living room. It made Sara smile instead of cry. The **next day** when Sara was eating lunch on the porch, she pretended to talk to Spark, so she wouldn't feel lonely. All of a sudden she stopped and listened. Sara could hear Spark barking. She **stood up** and **ran down** the steps, calling, "Here Spark! Here Spark! Where are you?" **Running** towards Sara, Spark barked, "Woof, Woof."*

Exercise

Add movement to a new story. Write about a family trip to the beach. You will have one main character and supporting characters. Move your characters from home to the beach. Move them—do not just plop them down at the beach. Take your readers on the trip with your characters. Let your readers experience what your characters see along the way. Tell your readers exactly how your characters feel when they reach the beach.

Turn your characters into birds. Have fun with your creativity. Bring in contrast, so you can move along fast and slow. The movement of each character can help develop his or her personality.

Worksheet

_____

_____

_____

_____

_____

_____

_____

_____

_____

_____

_____

_____

_____

_____

_____

_____

_____

_____

_____

Worksheet

_____

_____

_____

_____

_____

_____

_____

_____

_____

_____

_____

_____

_____

_____

_____

_____

_____

_____

_____

_____

Notes from the Author

Have you ever attended a lecture after a busy day at home or the office? Well, I have, and there is nothing more deadly than monotone in the lecturer's voice. It literally puts me to sleep! The same thing can happen when you write a story. You can literally put your audience to sleep. An occasional dynamic word will jar your reader back into your story flow.

Your words will do the work for you when used at the right time. Dynamic words are like speaking out loud or laughing. Their purpose is to keep your reader's attention. "Look at the **big** building!" or "Do you want a **big** piece of chocolate cake?" **Big** is a dynamic word and it has a very definite purpose.

The strength behind a dynamic word is the placement. It takes a writer who is sensitive to the reader's needs. Just keep in mind that a dynamic word is usually placed to hold your reader's attention until you can take their imagination into another dimension of your story.

Step Seven: Dynamic Words

Dynamic words are like a strong, powerful voice that will jolt the reader's interest. It only takes one word. In writing you do not have the sound of your voice to perk up your audience but you do have the power of words. It takes practice to use dynamic words at the right time.

Example

> Johnny **walked** out of the house, letting the door **close** behind him.

If I want my words to describe a very busy, energetic little boy, I would say:

> "Johnny **quickly** ran out of the house, letting the door **slam** behind him."

I now want to pick up momentum in the story. Which set of words should I use?

☞ *Run Johnny Run.*

☞ *Johnny, you had better go.*

In using **Run Johnny Run** I am using only three words, but they are dynamic enough to do the job.

Challenge yourself with this game each day. Write a sentence, but before you finish, select the most dynamic ending from at least four or five possible endings that you have created. For example, "Bobby didn't like going to school. One day instead of walking to the bus he…"

☞ ran and hid behind a tree   ☞ played sick

☞ ran to his grandmother   ☞ started to cry

I would select **ran and hid behind a tree** because it develops the personality and it leads the reader into anticipation of adventure.

Example

*Sara was a happy little girl until she **lost** Spark one day when she was out walking. Spark was her little dog. Spark was Sara's special friend. Spark kept Sara warm and cozy when the **cold wind blew** at night. Every day, Spark sat at Sara's feet while she ate her meals in the **big drafty** kitchen and sometimes in the big formal dining room. Sara **loved** Spark very much! Sara wasn't happy any more. Now Sara was **sad** and **alone** as she walked from room to room. Sara cried, "Oh Spark, where have you gone?"*

One day Sara thought she saw Spark sitting in her special chair in the living room. It made Sara *smile instead of cry. The next day when Sara was eating lunch on the porch, she pretended to talk to Spark, so she wouldn't feel lonely. All of a sudden she stopped and listened. Sara could hear Spark barking. She **stood up** and **ran down the steps,** calling, "Here Spark! Here Spark! Where are you?" **Running towards Sara,** Spark barked, "Woof, Woof."*

Exercise

Write one paragraph with dynamic words like the example. It is good writing practice and it will help to increase your vocabulary. A large vocabulary will make it easier to reduce your words when you start to edit.

Worksheet

_____

_____

_____

_____

_____

_____

_____

_____

_____

_____

_____

_____

_____

_____

_____

_____

_____

_____

_____

_____

_____

Worksheet

_____

_____

_____

_____

_____

_____

_____

_____

_____

_____

_____

_____

_____

_____

_____

_____

_____

_____

_____

_____

Notes from the Author

I have trouble remembering names, so I use a trick I saw in an article. The article suggested I associate names with a person, place, or thing in my past. The trick works except when a person's name does not reflect their personality. Then I find it difficult to call a person by their given name. I think of them as a Henry or Elizabeth, instead of Cody or Maria.

I know a person who has changed her name to change her luck. And it is common knowledge that actors and actresses often change their given names to professional names. There are also pen names instead of writers' real names.

With so many changes and uses of names it makes a person wonder what is the importance of a name. Actually, names trigger the mental image of the reader. They project a definite personality, place, and event in a story. Names complete the image that a writer develops and they are also an important part of the title. ❧

Step Eight: Names & Titles

Names should be easy to remember and fun to repeat, especially for children.

If you read the name Tiny Tim, would you visualize an overweight, muscular wrestler? No, you would visualize a very small person. Some names are sophisticated, others cute. There are even names that depict nationalities. In a story written about an Italian boy, would he be named **Fred**? No, **Tony** would be a better selection. It would reflect a more realistic Italian heritage.

When naming your characters, select names that will project the total personality. When a girl character is frail, shy, and blond, would you name her **Flame**? No, that name would be contradictory to the image the writer is trying to portray. The name **Mary** would be a better choice.

Fortunately, you can name your characters after their personalities have developed. Naming does not stop with just the characters. A town or event will also need names. The name itself can tell a story. If the story takes place in a happy village, **Sunny Village** would be more appropriate than **Gloomsville**.

The title of a story or book is the first thing a potential reader will see or hear. It is a powerful sales tool. It represents everything within the front and back cover. The title should reflect your story. "The Cry of the Wolf" is hardly a story about a New York City street. The title will draw readers to your story or book. Try to come up with something original and effective. The title can depict action, too.

There is also the subtitle. It is also very important as it will tell your reader, before they ever open the book, what they will gain from your story.

Example

> *The story about Sara and Spark could be named* ***Sara and Spark*** *or* ***My Friend Spark***. *My selection is* ***Sara and Spark***. *It is direct and simple and if a child wanted to call the story* ***Sara*** *or just* ***Spark***, *the story would still be identified.*
>
> *The subtitle is about* ***friendship***.

Exercise

Read ***Sara and Spark*** once again and list two or three titles and subtitles you would give it.

Titles:

> *1.*
>
> *2.*
>
> *3.*

Subtitles:

1.

2.

3.

Now select one of your stories and review the characters. Do the names depict their personalities? If you have any doubts about the names you have chosen, now is the time to compile a list of names. Ask your family or your friends what they think of the names. The final choice will be yours, of course, but be open to suggestions. Also select the title and subtitle for your story.

Title List

_____

_____

_____

_____

_____

_____

_____

_____

_____

_____

_____

_____

_____

_____

_____

_____

_____

_____

_____

_____

Sub-title List

_____

_____

_____

_____

_____

_____

_____

_____

_____

_____

_____

_____

_____

_____

_____

_____

_____

_____

_____

_____

_____

Notes from the Author

Details can be very boring. When listening to someone who is telling a story in detail, I always want to say "GET TO THE POINT!" And yet, I often find myself describing situations in great detail. You might call it habit or just the desire to get your point across.

I think of descriptive writing as detailed writing. When I have time to read a story by an author who writes with great detail, I enjoy it totally. It is seldom, however, that I have the time. Consequently I look for books that are few in words but grip my imagination from the first page.

When you think of children, they have very little time to just sit and listen unless you capture their imaginations. It is true that many writers, when writing for children, rely on illustrations to describe events and places. Although illustrations are a very big part of young children's books, it is the words that create your story.

When you submit your work to a publisher, your words are all they will see. When you are writing your book do not rely on anything but your creative words to keep the attention of your young reader. Think of illustrations or any other attribute as an enhancement.

Step Nine: Descriptive Writing

Up to this point, we have not worked on descriptive words. It is not because it is not important, but rather because all writers have their own unique style. This book is mainly for the purpose of letting creativity flow and no particular style of writing is discouraged.

Some writers go into a great deal of detail and others use dynamic words to take the place of descriptive writing.

The style of writing you use depends on the age of the readers. However, more and more I have students telling me their very young children prefer stories that are detailed with no pictures. But regardless of their preference, each word must be meaningful to hold the interest of your young reader or listener.

Example: Descriptive Writing

Johnny stood very quietly, leaning against the street light. His hands were cold. He tucked them under his arms to keep them warm. His ears were stinging from the cold wind whipping around the tall buildings. Johnny had nowhere to go. His big brown eyes were sad. His red hair hung limp. The worn soles of his shoes were lined with paper to keep his feet from touching the ground. He was standing on a deserted street. There was no sun, only gloom.

Example: Dynamic Words

Johnny was rigid. The fierce wind pierced his skin. Numbness encased him. He was destitute on a silent street.

Exercise

Try writing a descriptive story, one paragraph only. Then turn your story into a story of dynamic words, like the example above. It is good writing practice and it will help to increase your vocabulary.

Here are a few practice sentences.

1. *Mark was a busy boy. He couldn't sit still very long. He would run from room to room all day long.*

2. *Susan often sat by herself in the garden. She liked sitting among the flowers, looking at the sky, and feeling the silence around her.*

Reduce each sentence to six words.

1.

2.

Worksheet

_____

_____

_____

_____

_____

_____

_____

_____

_____

_____

_____

_____

_____

_____

_____

_____

_____

_____

_____

_____

Worksheet

_____

_____

_____

_____

_____

_____

_____

_____

_____

_____

_____

_____

_____

_____

_____

_____

_____

_____

Notes from the Author

When I am listening to another person talk, I hear what I want to hear and interpret the words into my own way of thinking. The person listening to me will do the same.

Socially we seldom select our words. We are too busy just conversing and that is all right, because there is still a chance to clear up any misunderstanding. We use facial expressions, tone of voice, or body language to get our message across. I, for one, always use my hands to emphasize my words.

In writing, however, there is no second chance. You rely solely on the choice of words and the correct punctuation and grammar to insure the interpretation you desire. In the creative process of writing, you are not concerned with grammar but once the story is complete, it must be reviewed and edited and made grammatically correct.

Editing will make your story stronger. It is the final step before sending it to a publisher or going to print if you are self-publishing. I recommend you have someone qualified, with an objective point of view, edit your story to give it the profession-alism you want to project to your readers. As the writer, you become too close to your creativity to see the obvious corrections needed.

Go back to one of your original stories, show it to others, and ask them to tell you about the story. Explain that it is just a draft and get their impression of what you are saying. There are times you will be disappointed in the response you receive and you will know you still have hours of rewriting to do.

In the final phase of editing it is tedious and time-consuming, but it is worth it. The extra work ensures that your story is presented in a professional way that is fulfilling for you and your readers.

Step Ten: Editing

Editing is important because it will tighten your story. Where you have used a paragraph, you can instead use two or three words to express the same thought. Write a paragraph, look at what you have written and ask yourself, "What did I say?" Then write it using two or three words. Be very selective with your words. Think of your words as dynamic and speaking for you on paper.

In editing you will not only take out words, but you will also change your words around to be more effective. You will have many edits before your story is ready to print. If your story is weak and your message is lost, it is often in the words or sentence structure. Take your time with editing; it is very important.

Proper editing can save you money when you go to print, if you are self-publishing. If a publishing house buys your story, their staff will give your story a final edit. When you edit your story, use the standard editing marks that you will find in the front or back of most dictionaries.

One of the most important steps in editing is correct spelling. If you hire an editor or proofreader, you should be able to rely on their expertise, but it is possible for a professional to miss an error. Ultimately your writing is your responsibility. Therefore, make your dictionary your best friend. It should be as close to you as your pen and paper or your computer. The most common dictionary is the *Webster's New World Dictionary of the American Language*. If you use a computer, there are programs that give you assistance in spelling and grammar, but only assistance.

The Tricky Dozen

The 12 most commonly misspelled words!

its	their	to	who's	your
it's	there	too	whose	you're
	they're	two		

If you want your words to say exactly what you mean, you must punctuate correctly. Improper punctuation will confuse the reader. A comma can change the whole meaning of a sentence.

Example

> 1. *Johnny, the boy next door, wants to play with you.*
>
> 2. *Johnny, the boy next door wants to play with you.*

Do you see the difference in meaning? In sentence one, Johnny is the boy next door. In sentence two, the boy next door, whose name we don't know, wants to play with Johnny.

Keep a copy of your first draft. In the editing process you often change what you originally wanted to say. It will save you time if you go back to your first draft and refresh your thoughts.

The following example has been edited. Compare the original example with the edited example that follows.

Example: Original

Sara was a happy little girl until she lost Spark one day when she was out walking. Spark was her little dog. Spark was Sara's special friend. Spark kept Sara warm and cozy when the cold wind blew at night. Every day, Spark sat at Sara's feet while she ate her meals in the big drafty kitchen and sometimes in the big formal dining room. Sara loved Spark very much! Sara wasn't happy any more. Now Sara was sad and alone as she walked from room to room. Sara cried, "Oh Spark, where have you gone?"

One day Sara thought she saw Spark sitting in her special chair in the living room. It made Sara smile instead of cry. The next day when Sara was eating lunch on the porch, she pretended to talk to Spark, so she wouldn't feel lonely. All of a sudden she stopped and listened. Sara could hear Spark barking. She stood up and ran down the steps, calling, "Here Spark! Here Spark! Where are you?" Running towards Sara, Spark barked, "Woof, Woof."

Example: Edited Copy

Sara was a happy little girl until she lost her dog Spark. Spark was Sara's special friend. Every night Spark kept Sara warm and cozy while she slept. Every day Spark sat at Sara's feet while she ate her meals in the big, drafty kitchen. Sara loved Spark very much! Now Sara was sad as she walked from room to room, all alone. Sara cried, "Oh Spark, where have you gone?" One day, Sara was eating lunch on the porch. She pretended to talk to Spark so she wouldn't feel lonely. All of a sudden, Sara could hear Spark barking! She stood up quickly, ran down the steps, and called, "Here Spark! Here Spark!" Spark barked, "Woof, woof." He ran out from behind the bushes, jumped on Sara and licked her face. Sara was so happy!

Exercise

For your next exercise, use a completed story. Choose one story you have written, review as needed, then develop your story by making sure all of the following elements are included:

☞ Main Character	☞ Contrast
☞ Message	☞ Movement
☞ Supportive Characters	☞ Dynamic Words
☞ Dialogue	☞ Names and Titles

Now it is time to start editing. You and another person should edit your story. Have your editing partner write comments in the margins of your story.

After reviewing the comments, change words around, replace words, punctuate, and make all the alterations that are needed to make your story complete.

You want your story to reach the emotions of the reader. Make sure you leave no words that will make it weak or boring. When you think you are ready to send your story to the publisher or the printer, put your story away for a few days. When you take it out again, give it another edit.

Final Editing

When I get ready to go shopping, I make sure I have everything I need. My arms and hands are always full of mail, books, or things to return. Just as I reach the door, I remember to go back into the kitchen to check the stove. Am I being overly cautious? Not really, I want to make sure everything is in order.

Trying to be perfect is very tedious and time consuming. In writing you want your final draft to be perfect and that takes one last look at your manuscript, after many edits. Editing is an ongoing process. Just when you think you have edited your story for the last time you will find something else to change. It could be punctuation, spelling, or the proper tense. A good friend can casually glance at your first page and say, "Uh, oh, typo!" Never let your manuscript leave your hands until it is letter perfect. It will then reflect professionalism.

The way you use your words will be your writing trademark. Do not change your unique style when you start your final editing.

The words must keep the interest of your reader. They must also move the reader along from page to page and, most important, they must do the job for you using the fewest words possible. You are writing for children. Be very direct. Keep in mind, the amount of words used in a story will change depending upon the age group of your reader.

If you have done your editing well, your words will trigger the imagination of the reader.

Notes from the Author

There are subjects that I find very difficult to write about, mainly because the subjects do not relate to my personal thoughts or actions. When I write with feelings and emotions, the words flow faster than I can type. But here I am trying to relate to the subject of layout.

Layout is a method I use to help with my editing, especially in reducing words. It helps me to see my story totally without turning pages. If I do not use a layout, I am continually turning back several pages to find what I have written or what names I have used.

Whenever I find a helping hand in writing, like laying out my story, I use it—especially when it enhances my creativity.

Step Eleven: Page Layout

Page layout is optional. However, I suggest you use it at least once to understand its value. In a creative layout you can see the flow of your whole story clearly, page by page, as it will appear in book form. This method works especially well when you want to tighten your story by reducing words or if you are writing a picture book.

The steps are simple and easy to follow. Review the following steps and examples before beginning your exercise.

Step 1:

Decide how many pages you want your book to contain. An average picture book contains approximately 30 –32 pages.

Step 2:

Make squares representing pages. The size of the square doesn't matter as long as it is easy for you to work with.

Step 3:

Take your story, as written, and place the sentences in the appropriate squares as you would like them to appear in your book. The actual text will begin on the right-hand side of your book. The words can be placed on the top, in the middle, or on the bottom of each page. You may even want your words to run across two pages. You can have one word on a page or even a page without words. A picture book often has pages with only illustrations. You will continue to edit and rearrange your words as you place them on your layout pages.

Step 4:

You will find that on some of the pages you will need to reduce your words. As you start to reduce your words keep the story line flowing smoothly.

Your completed layout will give you a clear, step-by-step picture of your book.

The following is an example of the previous steps. For my example I selected **Sara and Spark.** I decided to use fifteen pages of text for my story. The sample squares I selected are small but sufficient for the layout example. You may choose to use a much larger size. I put the sentences of my story on the appropriate pages and worked with the wording and layout until I was satisfied with the results.

Example

Sara was a happy little girl until she lost her dog Spark. Spark was Sara's special friend. Every night Spark kept Sara warm and cozy while she slept. Every day Spark sat at Sara's feet while she ate her meals in the big, drafty kitchen. Sara loved Spark very much! Now Sara was sad as she walked from room to room, all alone. Sara cried, "Oh Spark, where have you gone?" One day, Sara was eating lunch on the porch.

She pretended to talk to Spark so she wouldn't feel lonely. All of a sudden, Sara could hear Spark barking! She stood up quickly, ran down the steps, and called, "Here Spark! Here Spark!" Spark barked, "Woof, woof." He ran out from behind the bushes, jumped on Sara, and licked her face. Sara was so happy!

	1 Sara was a happy little girl until she lost her dog Spark.
2 Spark was Sara's special friend. Every night	3 Spark kept Sara warm and cozy while she slept.
4 Every day Spark sat at Sara's feet while she ate her meals in the big, drafty kitchen.	5 Sara loved Spark very much!
6 Now Sara was sad as she walked from room to room, all alone.	7 Sara cried, "Oh Spark, where have you gone?

8	9
One day, Sara was eating lunch on the porch.	She pretended to talk to Spark so she wouldn't feel lonely.

10	11
All of a sudden,	Sara could hear Spark barking!

12	13
She stood up quickly, ran down the steps, and called, "Here Spark! Here Spark!	Spark barked, "Woof, woof"

14	15
He ran out from behind the bushes, jumped on Sara, and licked her face.	Sara was so happy!

Exercise

Select the story you finalized with the editing steps given in the previous chapter. Using the steps given earlier, start your own layout.

Notes from the Author

There are times when I actually think I have a mental block. I just can't think of anything new or happy or sad or even beautiful to write about. I think I am at the end of my writing career! When a thought like that enters my mind I need to quickly jar my creativity into action.

To do this I use a special exercise that I have developed. I sit back, put my feet up, put a smile on my face, and hold a pen and paper in front of me. Then I follow the steps in the next chapter. Try not to think as you do it; just let your imagination write words for you in a very simple way.

This exercise is based on using color to inspire a picture and words. I have found that color is very important with creativity. If you are writing a Christmas story, try thinking of red, green, gold, or your favorite winter colors. Music will work as well.

In time you will devise your own exercises to encourage your creativity, but for now give my exercise a try.

Step Twelve: Creative Outline

When you have a mental block, use this color-based exercise to jump start your creativity. Let your ideas flow from the colors you choose. In the end, you will find that you have developed an outline for a new story, and you will take it from there.

Exercise

Inside each square, write a different color. Under each square, write either boy or girl; let the color motivate your decision. Then write a name for each character inspired by the color.

Inside the next two squares, write two different colors. Under each square, write an event that is inspired by the color of that square.

```
┌────────────────────┬────────────────────┐
│                    │                    │
│                    │                    │
│                    │                    │
│                    │                    │
└────────────────────┴────────────────────┘
```

Inside the next two squares, write two different colors. Then under each square, write the name of something that relates to nature and is inspired by the colors.

```
┌────────────────────┬────────────────────┐
│                    │                    │
│                    │                    │
│                    │                    │
│                    │                    │
└────────────────────┴────────────────────┘
```

Copy inside the following squares the **same colors in the same order** that you just wrote in the last six squares. Under the first two squares, write **geographical** areas inspired by the colors. Under the second two squares, write either **rich** or **poor,** as inspired by the color. Under the last two squares, write a **character trait** inspired by the color.

```
┌────────────────────┬────────────────────┐
│                    │                    │
│                    │                    │
│                    │                    │
│                    │                    │
└────────────────────┴────────────────────┘
```

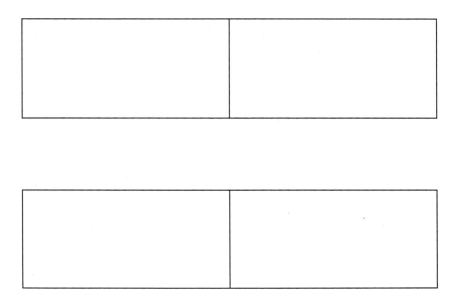

Using the outline you have just written, take each idea and write it in sequence on a piece of paper. Develop each idea into story form. You already have your characters' names, economic backgrounds, character traits, and events. It is up to you to select which character is a main character or a supporting character. Let the colors help you select.

Your message will form from this outline. Let your **creative ideas flow**. Create your story around your outline. You will be surprised how easy it will be. After you have written approximately two pages of free-flowing ideas; add contrast, dialogue, and movement, then edit your story. Last, but not least, lay out your story, continuing to edit as you do and remember to always:

☞ Enjoy your writing,

☞ Be original, and

☞ Your persistence will overcome all obstacles.

Glossary

Interpretation of Words

The interpretation of words in this glossary may not be found in the standard dictionary. They are the author's creative interpretations.

Acceptance: Thoughts that are understood and liked.

Achievement: You will gain by determination and diligent work.

Attribute: Significant words that highlight a story.

Bounds: Rigid guidelines limiting creativity.

Carry: A vehicle supporting a message.

Childhood: The young years of the writer.

Communicate: The writer relays ideas through writing.

Contrast: Showing a difference to heighten the reader's interest.

Creativity: A unique imagination that is used to write stories.

Conflict: A difference in personalities, opinions, and situations.

Creator: Person who develops an image or thought for the enjoyment of others.

Descriptive Writing: A detailed account of the story.

Dialogue: A way of speaking to develop a personality.

Dynamic Word: Specific word to draw the attention or interest of the reader.

Editing: An essential step in completing a story.

Emphasis: A particular importance given to an aspect of the story.

Exercise: A helpful step in developing a writing skill.

Feeling: A personal experience or knowledge of an actual response.

Final Editing: The final step in the completion of a manuscript.

Flow: Continuous movement of words.

Forceful: Exceptional words projecting an image, event, or action in a story.

Freedom: Releasing your thoughts without inhibitions.

Glossary: The writer's interpretation of words.

Grown-up: Older in numerical age.

Idea: A picture in a mind.

Imagination: An individual place to develop ideas.

Important: A significant impression of words.

Learn: Growth in writing knowledge.

Main Character: The principal part of a story and the message carrier.

Make-believe: An individual space of fun.

Material: Information accumulated by the writer.

Mental Block: A temporary void of creative thoughts.

Mental Picture: Imaginary story formed in a writer's mind.

Message: An experience or thought a writer shares with the reader.

Motivates: Words that help to arouse the reader's emotions.

Movement: A tool that helps to keep a story interesting.

Opportunity: A chance to expand your creativity.

Option: A writer's choice.

Organize: A systematic planning of ideas.

Outline: A number of events to follow when writing a story.

Page Layout: Page-by-page view of story or illustrations.

Perseverance: Go on in spite of difficulties.

Personality: An entity developed through the writer's imagination.

Picture Book: Words coordinated with pictures, for very young children.

Plop: Lack of continuous movement.

Rejection: The writer's feeling of not being accepted.

Review: An objective opinion about a book.

Rule: An established guide to follow.

Sale: A book ready for market.

Simple: An uncomplicated and easy method of writing.

Skill: A learned or gifted talent.

Stagnant: No movement or contrast.

Step: A simple method leading to a result.

Stimulate: Words that provoke a reader's reaction to a story.

Story: A statement created by a writer.

Strategy: A writer's plan or method for achieving an end.

Style: A unique trademark

Text: The written words on a page.

Tighten: Reducing, replacing, or rearranging words in a manuscript.

Thinker: Capable of forming a mental picture.

Thought: An idea.

Unique: One-of-a-kind, a special talent.

Verbally: When expressing thoughts through oral communications.

Visualize: A mental picture before it is put on paper.

Written Form: When words form a message on paper.

Writers Group: The published and non-published writers.

Wilt: To lose freshness from lack of water.

Index

Order Form

Fax orders: (480) 596-4037
Telephone orders: (480) 905-0337
On-line orders: vrpub@uswest.net
Postal orders: VR Publications
                          PO Box 4643
                          Scottsdale, AZ 85261

_____ *Young at Heart: The Step-By-Step Way of* $12.95 ea. $_____
              Writing Children's Stories

Arizona residents add sales tax 7.1% (.92 cents per book) $_____

SHIPPING & HANDLING
$3.50 for the first book and $2.00 for each additional book $_____

                                                           Total $_____

Payment: Check or money order payable to: VR Publications.

_____ Please send titles and prices of other books available.

Ship To:

Name:_____

Street:_____

City:_____

State:_____Zip:_____

Daytime Phone (_____) _____

E-mail Address:_____

Is this a gift?   ❑   Yes   ❑   No